CLASSIC CANDY

CLASSIC CANDY

Old-Style Fudge, Taffy, Caramel Corn, and Dozens of Other Treats for the Modern Kitchen

ABIGAIL R. GEHRING

Skyhorse Publishing

Skyhorse Publishing books may be purchased in bulk at special discounts
for sales promotion, corporate gifts, fund-raising, or educational
purposes. Special editions can also be created to specifications. For details,
contact the Special Sales Department, Skyhorse Publishing, 307 West 36th
Street, 11th Floor, New York, NY 10018 or info@skyhorsepublishing.com.

Skyhorse® and Skyhorse Publishing® are registered trademarks of Skyhorse
Publishing, Inc.®, a Delaware corporation.

Visit our website at www.skyhorsepublishing.com.

10 9 8 7 6 5 4 3 2 1

Library of Congress Cataloging-in-Publication Data is available on file.
ISBN: 978-1-62636-005-1

Printed in China

{ Contents }

Introduction   vi

A Few Notes on Tools   viii

Ingredients   x

All About Chocolate   xv

Candy Temperature Chart   xxi

Chocolate, Fudge, and Candy Bars   1

Taffy, Toffee, and Caramels   33

Hard Candies, Brittles, and Bark   49

Soft Candies, Marshmallows, and Meringues   65

Fruits, Nuts, and other Sweetmeats   91

Resources   111

Recipe Index   113

Food Allergy Index   115

Conversion Charts   118

{ Introduction }

Growing up, we rarely had candy in the house. Pies and cookies on special occasions, yes, and chocolate chips stashed in the cupboard, but I honestly can't remember seeing a candy wrapper in the house for the first twelve or so years of my life. Probably because of that, I seldom craved candy—except chocolate, lots of chocolate—as an adult. That is, until I tried making candy at home. While the occasional store-bought candy I tried tasted fake and uninspired, the confections that came from my kitchen surprised me with their rich flavors and satisfying textures. Peppermint patties that had the fresh, crisp bite of a wintery morning; salted caramels that dissolved in buttery bliss on my tongue; candy corn that actually had flavor!

I had discovered a whole new, delightful culinary genre. The only problem was that at the same time that I was discovering the joys of homemade candy, I was also discovering that my body does not respond well to dairy or sugar (I had long since discovered that gluten was a problem). So there I was, in the middle of writing a cookbook on candy, and trying my darndest to avoid all sugar and dairy products, which meant depending almost entirely on family and coworkers to taste test my creations. As I lamented this ironic situation to friends, more and more folks told me that they, too, were unable to properly digest and metabolize sugar, gluten, dairy, or some combination of those things. I decided it was time for a little further experimentation. As a result, you'll see that many of the recipes in this book include notes for ways to make these candies dairy-free, and/or gluten-free, and I've included a section on alternative sweeteners (page xi).

That said, people don't eat candy to be healthy! Candy is an indulgence, a celebration of life's sweetness, and for many people a reminder of childhood pleasures. I hope that the candies in this book evoke memories of colorful candy shops, carnivals, and birthday parties. And I hope they inspire more people to create new memories of cooking with friends and family and experimenting with all the colors, flavors, and textures involved in making candy.

—Abigail R. Gehring

"It is the sweet, simple things in life which are the real ones after all."
—Laura Ingalls Wilder

{ A Few Notes on Tools }

The recipes in this book are of the old-fashioned sort—simple, classic recipes that don't require fancy equipment or even any special molds. You should be able to make anything you see here with the tools you already have in your kitchen. There are a few tools that will make some of these recipes much easier, though. If you don't have them, they may be worth investing in.

Double Boiler

Because chocolate is very sensitive and only likes to be melted *very slowly*, double boilers are a helpful tool. If you don't have one and don't feel like getting one, you can devise your own by placing a heatproof glass bowl over the top of a saucepan with a little water in the bottom. Just make sure the water doesn't touch the bottom of the bowl.

Candy Thermometer

You don't absolutely have to have a candy thermometer to succeed in candy-making, but for about $10 you can take most of the guesswork out of the process. For hard candies, taffy, toffee, and many of the other recipes in this book, you'll need to heat sugar mixtures to a fairly specific temperature to achieve the desired consistency in your final product. Your grandmother may have used the hard ball/soft ball method to determine candy temperatures without a thermometer, and certainly you can, too (see chart on page xxi). But you could also buy a cheap thermometer and save yourself the hassle of sticky syrup dripped all over your countertop and the stress of guesstimating the relative density of a ball of liquefied sugar.

Food Processor

Though more of an investment than a candy thermometer, a food processor is also good for many more kitchen purposes. Once you own one you'll find yourself using it for almost anything you prepare, from pie dough to chopped salads to homemade nut butters. In terms of candy, it's wonderful for recipes that call for chopped fruit or nuts. If you don't have one you can, of course, use a knife to chop dried fruits. For nuts, you can put them in a plastic bag and run a rolling pin over the bag to crush the nuts into small pieces.

Parchment Paper vs. Waxed Paper

Parchment paper is coated with silicone, whereas waxed paper is coated with wax (duh). When waxed paper gets hot, the wax melts and can seep into your food. Thus, I recommend using parchment paper instead of waxed paper for most recipes. Try to find unbleached parchment paper (available at many health food stores, or see online resources on page 111), since the bleach used in the white parchment paper is mildly toxic. Okay, so it's not going to kill you . . . probably, at least right away . . . but you might as well be as healthy as you can be (while eating candy)!

{ Ingredients }

You won't have a hard time finding the ingredients you need for these recipes in your local grocery store. But read these notes anyway if you're interested in learning a bit more about what's going into your delicious treats. Warning: this section may make you think about certain ingredients in a new way that will be rather inconvenient. Yes, I know, this is a candy book, not some sort of hippy, earthy, crunchy health food book. But I happen to think that health-conscious folks should be able to enjoy sweet treats, and one of the advantages of making your own candies is that you can choose ingredients that are healthier than what you'd buy off a candy shelf at the store.

Sugar

You'll find granulated sugar, brown sugar (light and dark), and confectioners' sugar in the recipes that follow. If the recipe just says "sugar," I mean regular old granulated sugar, which could be the white stuff you're used to or the unbleached raw granulated sugar. Either will be just fine. If you're in the middle of making a recipe and discover you're all out of brown sugar or confectioners' sugar (also called "powdered sugar"), you can make your own using these equivalents:

1 cup brown sugar = 1 cup granulated sugar + 1 tablespoon molasses

1 cup confectioners' sugar = 1 cup granulated sugar + 1 tablespoon cornstarch, whirled in a food processor or blender until mixture becomes powdery.

Alternative Sweeteners

If you're diabetic or just prefer not to spike your blood sugar through the roof, there are sugar substitutes available, and some are quite good.

Stevia is an herb that's been used as a sweetener in South America for centuries. It's suitable for diabetics and those looking to keep their weight in check. It does leave a strange aftertaste, which some people (myself included) find difficult to get past. Stevia does not caramelize like regular sugar, so it is not an acceptable sugar substitute for hard candies, caramel, or taffy. It's also much sweeter than regular sugar, so you only need about 1 teaspoon of stevia for every 1 cup of sugar called for in a recipe.

Swerve is relatively new to the market, but it's getting lots of great reviews. I tried it for the first time while working on this book, and it really does taste like regular sugar! It's a sugar alcohol, like xylitol, only it doesn't have the digestive side-effects typical of xylitol. It's safe for diabetics and contains no calories, there's no weird aftertaste, and it's the same sweetness as sugar, so it has a 1:1 ratio to sugar called for in recipes. It does caramelize, so it can be used in hard candies, taffy, etc. It's available in granulated form or in confectioners' sugar form. If you can't find it in your local health food store, you can order from www.swervesweetener.com.

Corn Syrup and Brown Rice Syrup

Corn syrup is sugar from corn, in syrup form. But you knew that already. What you might not realize is that most corn syrup is made from genetically modified (GM) corn. GMOs (genetically modified organisms) are banned or are required to be labeled in more than sixty countries around the world because there is evidence that they contribute to a wide range of health problems (I won't get on my soap box here, but you should do a little research). The good news is, you can buy organic corn syrup, which is not made from GM corn. See the resource section on page 111 for more information.

Why not just skip corn syrup altogether? Because corn syrup lends a unique texture to candy that is hard to obtain from other sugars or syrups.

The closest alternative I've found is brown rice syrup, which is less sweet than corn syrup and has a distinct flavor, but it functions similarly to corn syrup in most recipes. You can find it in health food stores, or see the resource section of this book (page 111).

Honey, Maple Syrup, and Agave

Honey and maple syrup are great for use in dried fruit and nut candies, but they don't caramelize enough for use in hard candies, caramels, or taffy. They all will raise your blood sugar, so if you're diabetic, these natural sugars are not a safe alternative to processed sugar for you. However, they are less refined than granulated cane sugar and have some health benefits—especially honey. As for agave, I wouldn't bother with it, for the reasons outlined below.

The best honey—both for nutrition and flavor—is in its raw form. Raw honey is a powerful antioxidant and has antiviral antibacterial, and antifungal properties. It strengthens the immune system and can fight allergies (particularly if the honey is from local bees).

Maple syrup is, well, *delicious*. I'm from Vermont, so I grew up tapping trees and boiling down the sap to make our liquid gold. We used to drink it when it was halfway done—still a little watery, but delightfully sweet—in little shot glasses. Maple syrup doesn't rank quite as high as honey on the health scorecard but it does have a lot of anti-inflammatory and antioxidant properties.

Agave, sometimes called "the great Mexican aloe," produces a sweet sap, or nectar, that is traditionally extracted from the leaves, filtered, and heated to become a concentrated syrup—sort of like the tropical version of maple syrup. Sounds great, right? There's a hitch. Most agave sweeteners you can find in stores comes from the blue agave plant, and rather than the sap being extracted from the leaves, it comes from the starchy root bulb. The agave glucose is converted to syrup through an enzymatic and chemical process that is similar to how cornstarch is converted to high fructose corn syrup (HFCS). And if you didn't know, HFCS messes with your hormones

and makes you fat. I'm not a doctor, but unless you're going to go pick an agave leaf and extract the sap yourself, I'd stay away from it.

Sweetened Condensed Milk

Sweetened condensed milk makes lots of candy recipes super quick and easy. If you don't have any on hand, or don't like some of the ingredients used in store-bought varieties, you can make your own. It takes a while, though. (I also recently found organic sweetened condensed milk at Trader Joe's—exciting!) The below recipe makes about 14 ounces, the equivalent of 1 store-bought can of sweetened condensed milk.

1½ cups whole milk or full-fat coconut milk

½ cup sugar

3 tablespoons butter or coconut oil

1 teaspoon vanilla

Combine milk and sugar in a saucepan over very low heat and stir until melted. Allow to simmer, uncovered, for about 2 hours, stirring occasionally. When reduced by about half, add the butter and vanilla and remove from heat. Allow to cool and then use immediately or store in a glass jar.

Butter

If you don't have an issue with dairy products, use real, unsalted butter when a recipe calls for butter. The flavor and texture will be your reward. However, if you're steering clear of dairy for any reason, coconut oil is a good alternative (you'll see it used in many recipes in this book). I don't recommend margarine for making candy, since texture is so important, but if you have your heart set on it, choose a variety that doesn't contain hydrogenated oils.

Chocolate

Chocolate deserves a section all unto itself. Keep reading.

{ All About Chocolate }

Chocolate, as far as I'm concerned, is one of God's greatest gifts to humanity. Delicious, mood-enhancing, and with some redeeming health qualities (love those antioxidants!), it's hard to imagine a more perfect treat.

Types of Chocolate

You can use just about any kind of chocolate for the recipes in this book. Sometimes I suggest semisweet or dark, but feel free to use whatever kind you prefer. Here's a brief breakdown:

Milk Chocolate: Contains 10–20% cocoa solids and more than 12% milk solids.

Dark Chocolate: May contain up to 12% milk solids and has a high cocoa solids content. Dark chocolate is sort of an umbrella category that includes sweet, semisweet, bittersweet, or unsweetened chocolate.

Semisweet chocolate: Usually contains 40–60% cocoa solids. Most chocolate chips are semisweet.

Melting Chocolate vs. Tempering Chocolate

Tempering chocolate is rarely, if ever, really necessary for homemade confections. So feel free to skip this section and just read the tips on melting chocolate below. That said, tempering chocolate will give your chocolate-covered candies a glossier, harder, and more professional-looking finish. I rarely take the extra time to do it—I didn't temper the chocolate used in any of the candies photographed for this book—but really, it's not that much more work. Basically, you melt some chocolate, remove from heat, add some more chocolate, and stir like your life depends on it. The chocolate will not taste any different, but it will look more polished when set and will take longer to melt on your fingertips.

Here's the science behind tempering chocolate. The cocoa butter in chocolate is a hard-saturated fat, so it's made up of a bunch of very tiny crystals. When chocolate is heated above 91.5 degrees, those little crystals break down, which creates melted chocolate. When the chocolate cools to about 80 degrees, the molecules come back together, but they're not in the same crystallized shape they were before you heated it up. By heating and cooling the chocolate at specific temperatures, you can control what types of crystals your chocolate ends up with. Tempering is a specific method of heating and cooling that leads to "beta crystals," which create a chocolate finish that is shiny, smooth, and will crack if you tap it with your fingernail.

Before reading about how to temper chocolate, there are a couple things you should know:

If you're using chocolate chips, don't bother tempering. In fact, you *can't* temper chocolate chips, or any chocolate that has added ingredients like soy lecithin or vanilla extract. Only temper if you're using a block of high quality chocolate.

If you're going to be coating the chocolate with crushed nuts, coconut, or anything else, don't bother tempering. You'll be covering up your glossy chocolate finish anyway.

Tempering Chocolate

Tools

1. Double boiler, or a saucepan with a glass or ceramic heatproof bowl that fits snugly in the top.
2. Candy thermometer
3. Rubber spatula

Directions

Chop the chocolate into evenly sized small pieces.

Fill the bottom of the double-boiler to just below the bottom of the top piece or the bowl—the bottom of the bowl should not be touching the water. Heat the water to simmering.

Place ⅔ of the chocolate pieces in the top of the double-boiler and stick the candy thermometer in the side. Stir occasionally as the chocolate melts. Dark chocolate should be removed from the heat when it reaches 115°F. Milk or white chocolate should be removed at 110°F. Wipe the moisture from the bottom of the bowl after removing it from the double boiler.

Immediately stir the melted chocolate with your spatula. Stir fast and furiously! Add the remaining ⅓ of your chocolate gradually, continuing to stir. It'll take about 15 minutes for the chocolate to get down to the desired temperature: 90°F for dark chocolate, or 88°F for milk or white chocolate.

To test the chocolate, dip a metal knife into the chocolate and refrigerate it for a couple minutes (give it an extra minute or two for milk or white chocolate). If, when you remove it from the fridge, it's hard and glossy, you've done it! If it's still sticky or looks streaky, then keep stirring your chocolate for another few minutes and test again.

CHOCOLATE + WATER = BAD

Chocolate and water do not like each other. Whether you're tempering your chocolate or just melting it, make sure all your utensils are completely dry. If you get even a drop or two of water in the chocolate, it may seize up, becoming chunky and useless for dipping purposes. If this happens, use the chocolate in something baked (like brownies) or place it in hot milk for a rich hot chocolate and start over with new chocolate for your confections.

TIPS FOR MELTING CHOCOLATE

- Chop the chocolate in even pieces.
- Make sure bowl and utensils are dry.

Melting in the microwave

- Use a microwave-safe bowl.
- Set the microwave to 50% power if possible.
- Plan 1 minute for 1 ounce of chocolate, 3 minutes for 8 oz, 3.5 minutes for 1 lb.

Melting on the stovetop

- Any metal or glass bowl that fits snugly in the top of a saucepan will work if you don't have an actual double boiler.
- Melt over low heat and stir slowly, gently, and constantly.
- A rubber spatula works best for stirring.

{ Candy Temperature Chart }

If you don't have a candy thermometer, you can test if your sugar mixture is at the right temperature by dropping a bit of syrup from a spoon into a glass of very cold water and watching what happens.

Thread	begins at 230°	**Syrup Stage** When the syrup is drizzled from a spoon, it forms a very fine thread.
Soft Ball	begins at 234°	**Fudge, Penuche, Cream Fillings** When a small amount of syrup is dropped into cold water it forms a ball that can easily be flattened when pinched.
Firm Ball	begins at 244°	**Caramels** When a small amount of syrup is dropped into cold water it forms a ball that has resistance when pinched. It's still sticky.
Hard Ball	begins at 250°	**Taffy and Marshmallows** When a small amount of syrup is dropped into cold water it forms a ball that is firm but still pliable.
Soft Crack	begins at 270°	**Butterscotch (slightly chewy)** When a small amount of syrup is dropped into cold water it forms thin, pliable threads.
Hard Crack	300°–310°	**Hard Candies, Brittles, and Toffee** When a small amount of syrup is dropped into cold water it forms hard, brittle threads.

{ Chocolate, Fudge, and Candy Bars }

Chocolate Coconut Candy Bars	2
Chocolate-Dipped Honeycomb	4
Chocolate Peanut Butter Balls	5
Peanut Butter Cups	6
Chocolate-Dipped Pretzel Rods	8
Dream Bars	9
Cherry Cordials	10
Mocha Fudge	12
Peanut Butter Fudge	14
White Chocolate Peppermint Fudge	15
Truffles	16
Coconut Milk Truffles	18
Hazelnut Rocher Truffles	20
Chocolate Cheesecake Bon Bons	21
Peppermint Patties	22
Coconut Oil Peppermint Patties	24
Orange Creams	26
Penuchi	28
Chocolate Caramel Peanut Butter Candy Bars	29

Chocolate Coconut Candy Bars

A chewy coconut filling coated in rich chocolate . . . mmm. For a variation, press a whole almond into the top of each coconut rectangle before dipping the candies in chocolate.

MAKES ABOUT 36 CANDY BARS.

Ingredients

---

14 ounces coconut flakes

2 cups confectioners' sugar

¼ teaspoon salt

1 teaspoon vanilla

1 can sweetened condensed milk

1 pound dark chocolate, chopped or 16 ounces chocolate chips

1 tablespoon corn or coconut oil

Directions

1. In a large bowl mix together the coconut, confectioners' sugar, salt, vanilla, and condensed milk.
2. Line a 7" × 10" baking pan with foil. Press the coconut mixture into the pan evenly and refrigerate for about an hour.
3. Remove from the refrigerator and slice into 1" × 2" rectangles.
4. Place the chocolate in a saucepan over low heat, add the oil, and stir until melted and smooth. Spear each coconut bar with a fork and dip in chocolate to coat, then set back on the foil-lined baking pan. Refrigerate for at least 10 minutes before enjoying.

Chocolate-Dipped Honeycomb

Dipping honeycomb candies in chocolate helps to seal out moisture so that they maintain their chewy texture for longer. A 9" x 13" pan will yield candies that are about ½" thick. If you like your candies thicker or thinner, adjust the pan size.

MAKES ABOUT 60 PIECES.

Ingredients

¼ cup honey	1 cup brown sugar
½ cup light corn syrup	1 tablespoon baking soda
1 cup granulated sugar	12 ounces dark chocolate

Directions

1. Line a cookie sheet or 9" × 13" pan with parchment paper or foil and brush lightly with butter or oil.

2. In a large saucepan, combine honey, corn syrup, and granulated and brown sugar. Be sure the pan is large enough for the mixture to triple in size as it cooks. Keep your candy thermometer in the mixture and watch as the temperature rises and the mixture transforms from liquid to foam. No need to stir.

3. When the mixture reaches 300°F, remove from heat and add the baking soda. Whisk the mixture and watch as it foams wildly. Keep whisking for about a minute, and then pour onto the parchment paper–lined pan. Allow to cool for about an hour and then break into pieces.

4. Melt chocolate in a double boiler. You can dip a corner of each piece of honeycomb in the chocolate or fully submerge the pieces. Place chocolate-coated honeycomb on another cookie sheet lined with parchment paper to dry. Store in the refrigerator.

Chocolate Peanut Butter Balls

Peanut butter and chocolate is my favorite food combination, though these candies are also delicious made with almond or cashew butter. You can substitute the butter for coconut oil to make these dairy-free. To keep them gluten-free, use gluten-free rice cereal or gluten-free graham crackers.

MAKES ABOUT 4 DOZEN BALLS.

Ingredients

2 cups creamy peanut butter

½ cup butter

½ teaspoon vanilla

4 cups confectioners' sugar

2 cups crisp rice cereal or graham cracker crumbs

2 cups semisweet chocolate chips

Directions

1. In a large saucepan over low heat, combine peanut butter, butter, and vanilla. Heat and stir until thoroughly mixed.
2. Remove from heat and add sugar and cereal or graham cracker crumbs. Stir to combine, cover, and place in refrigerator for half an hour or more.
3. Remove dough from refrigerator and roll into small balls. Place on a parchment paper–lined cookie sheet.
4. In a double boiler, melt the chocolate chips. Roll the balls in the chocolate and return to the parchment paper. Store in refrigerator.

Peanut Butter Cups

Use any kind of chocolate you like for these candies. To make these dairy-free, substitute the butter for coconut oil.

Ingredients

1 cup smooth peanut butter	¼ teaspoon salt
3 tablespoons unsalted butter, room temperature	12 ounces chocolate, chopped
	24 foil candy cups
½ cup confectioners' sugar	Pastry brush

Directions

1. Mix together the peanut butter and softened butter until smooth. Add the confectioners' sugar and salt and mix.

2. Melt the chocolate in a double boiler or in the microwave. Remove from heat and use a teaspoon to drop a little melted chocolate in the bottom of each candy cup. Use the brush to "paint" the inside sides of the cups with chocolate.

3. Scoop a little of the peanut butter mixture into each cup, and then top with more melted chocolate. Refrigerate until set.

Chocolate-Dipped Pretzel Rods

Homemade candies don't get much easier than this. Once rolled in sprinkles, nuts, coconut flakes, or other small candies, these are the perfect party treat! Serve them in a tall glass or vase, or package them individually in cellophane with a ribbon tied around the base.

MAKES 24 PRETZEL RODS.

Ingredients

12 ounces chocolate, chopped

24 pretzel rods

Assorted sprinkles, coarse sugar, crushed nuts, or other garnishes

Directions

1. Melt the chocolate in a double boiler.
2. Dip each pretzel rod in the chocolate, roll in desired garnish, and place on a parchment–lined cookie sheet to set. Refrigerate for about 30 minutes before serving.

Dream Bars

As far as I'm concerned, these have all the makings of a perfect candy bar—chocolate, nuts, and coconut! To make these dairy-free and vegan, replace the butter with coconut oil and replace the eggs with 2 tablespoons ground flaxseeds mixed with 6 tablespoons water until it becomes gelatinous.

MAKES ABOUT 24 SQUARES.

Ingredients

½ cup butter, softened	2 teaspoons vanilla
1 cup all-purpose flour	1½ cups coconut flakes
1½ cups light brown sugar	2 tablespoons flour
½ teaspoon salt	⅛ teaspoon salt
2 eggs	1 cup chopped nuts
½ teaspoon baking powder	1 cup mini chocolate chips

Directions

1. Grease a 10" × 10" baking pan. Preheat oven to 350°F.
2. Beat together the softened butter, ½ cup brown sugar, 1 cup flour, and ½ teaspoon salt. Press into the bottom of the greased baking pan. Bake about 10 minutes, or until just barely brown.
3. In a mixing bowl, stir together 2 tablespoons flour, remaining 1 cup brown sugar, ⅛ teaspoon salt, and baking powder. Beat together the eggs and vanilla and then add to dry ingredients and mix.
4. Pour wet mixture over the baked crust. Sprinkle coconut flakes and chocolate chips evenly over the top.
5. Bake for 20–25 minutes. Cut into squares while still warm.

Cherry Cordials

These cherry cordials got rave reviews at my last family gathering. Packaged in a box or small tin, they make a great holiday or hostess gift. Substitute the butter for coconut oil to make these dairy-free.

MAKES 30 CANDIES.

Ingredients

---

30 maraschino cherries, stems removed

1½ tablespoons butter, softened

2 tablespoons corn syrup

1½ cups confectioners' sugar

2 teaspoons vodka or cherry schnapps

8 ounces chocolate, chopped

Directions

1. In a medium-size bowl, mix together the butter, corn syrup, and vodka or schnapps. Add the confectioners' sugar and mix until smooth.

2. Drain the cherries. Form a ball of confectioners' sugar dough around each cherry, rolling between your palms to make it smooth. Place on a parchment paper–lined cookie sheet and chill in the refrigerator for about 30 minutes.

3. Melt the chocolate in a double boiler. Use a spoon to roll each ball in the melted chocolate. Place on the parchment paper-lined cookie sheet to set. Refrigerate for 30 minutes or so before serving. Store in the refrigerator.

Mocha Fudge

Making fudge is so easy! To make your own sweetened condensed milk
(out of cow's milk or coconut milk), see page xiv.

MAKES ABOUT 16 SQUARES.

Ingredients

1 14-ounce can sweetened con- densed milk	½ teaspoon vanilla
12 ounces semisweet chocolate chips	1 teaspoon instant coffee granules

Directions

1. Grease an 8" × 8" baking pan.
2. In a medium saucepan, heat sweetened condensed milk and chocolate chips. Stir and heat until mixture becomes smooth. Remove
from heat and add vanilla and instant coffee granules.
3. Pour into pan and allow to cool until set. Slice into 1" squares.

Peanut Butter Fudge

This fudge is ridiculously easy to make. To make it dairy-free, use coconut milk instead of cow's milk. Either chunky or smooth peanut butter will work just fine.

MAKES ABOUT 16 SQUARES.

Ingredients

2 cups sugar	1 cup peanut butter
½ cup milk	1 teaspoon vanilla

Directions

1. Grease an 8" × 8" baking pan.
2. In a medium saucepan, bring sugar and milk to a boil. Allow to boil for about 2½ minutes, stirring regularly, and then remove from heat. Add the peanut butter and vanilla and stir until mixed.
3. Pour into pan and allow to cool until set. Slice into 1" squares.

White Chocolate Peppermint Fudge

This fudge looks as festive as it tastes! If you're feeling really ambitious, make your own sweetened condensed milk (page xiv) and your own peppermint candy canes (page 60)! To make these dairy-free and vegan, use coconut sweetened condensed milk and coconut oil instead of butter.

MAKES ABOUT 16 SQUARES.

Ingredients

18 ounces white chocolate chips

1 14-ounce can sweetened condensed milk

¼ cup salted butter, cut into tablespoons

1 teaspoon peppermint oil or vanilla extract

1 cup crushed peppermint sticks (about 10 candy canes)

Directions

1. Line an 8" × 8" baking pan with parchment paper. You can cut the paper at the corners of the pan to avoid wrinkles.
2. Place the white chocolate chips, condensed milk, and butter in a double boiler and melt over low heat, stirring constantly. Remove from heat and add peppermint oil or vanilla extract and ½ cup of the crushed peppermint sticks.
3. Pour the mixture into the lined pan and sprinkle the remaining ½ cup crushed peppermint sticks over the top.
4. Chill in the refrigerator for about 2 hours before cutting into small squares to serve.

Truffles

Truffles are fun to make because there's so much room for creativity! Choose your favorite flavorings and coatings and go to town.

MAKES 35 TRUFFLES.

Ingredients

12 ounces semisweet or dark chocolate, chopped into small pieces	1 teaspoon vanilla
½ cup heavy cream	Cocoa powder, crushed nuts, or coconut flakes for coating

Directions

1. Place the chocolate pieces in a medium-size mixing bowl.
2. In a small saucepan, heat the cream until it begins to simmer, and then pour over the chocolate. Add the vanilla and stir until the mixture becomes smooth. Refrigerate for about 2 hours.
3. Line a baking sheet with parchment paper. Remove the ganache mixture from the refrigerator. Scoop out small spoonfuls of the ganache and then roll between your palms to form smooth balls. Place on the lined baking sheet and refrigerate for another 30 minutes.
4. Roll the balls in the coating of your choice and serve. Store in the refrigerator in an airtight container.

TRUFFLE ADDITIONS

Add any of the following to your ganache along with (or instead of) the vanilla:

Mocha: 1 tablespoon coffee liqueur and/or 1 tablespoon instant coffee granules

Nutty: 2 tablespoons nut butter

Spicy: ¼ teaspoon cayenne pepper and/or 1 teaspoon cinnamon

Citrus: 1 teaspoon orange or lemon zest

Coconut Milk Truffles

These rich truffles are dairy-free, as long as you choose chocolate that doesn't contain any dairy.

MAKES ABOUT 30 TRUFFLES.

Ingredients

---

10 ounces semisweet or dark chocolate, chopped in small bits

1 cup (about ½ can) full-fat coconut milk

2 tablespoons coconut oil

1 teaspoon vanilla

½ teaspoon cinnamon

Cocoa powder, crushed nuts, or coconut flakes for coating

Directions

1. Place the chocolate pieces in a medium-size mixing bowl.
2. In a small saucepan, heat the coconut milk and the coconut oil until it begins to simmer, and then pour over the chocolate. Add the vanilla and cinnamon and stir until the mixture becomes smooth. Refrigerate for about 2 hours.
3. Line a baking sheet with parchment paper. Remove the ganache mixture from the refrigerator. Scoop out small spoonfuls of the ganache and then roll between your palms to form smooth balls. Place on the lined baking sheet and refrigerate for another 30 minutes.
4. Roll the balls in the coating of your choice and serve. Store in the refrigerator in an airtight container.

Hazelnut Rocher Truffles

Rich and with that perfect bit of crunchy texture, these have long been one of my favorites. You can substitute the cookies with rice crispies or corn flakes to make these gluten-free.

MAKES ABOUT 50 TRUFFLES.

Ingredients

2 cups crushed vanilla wafer cookies or hazelnut wafer cookies	1 cup Nutella
	¼ cup hazelnut liqueur (optional)
2 cups toasted hazelnuts	8 ounces dark chocolate, chopped

Directions

1. In a food processor, pulverize the cookies and hazelnuts. Add the Nutella and liqueur and pulse until mixed.

2. Refrigerate mixture for about 20 minutes. When firm enough to handle, form into bite-size balls. Place on a parchment paper–lined baking sheet and freeze for 10 to 15 minutes.

3. In a double boiler, melt the chocolate. Dip each ball in the chocolate and set on the lined tray to set. Refrigerate another 10 minutes or so before serving. Store in the refrigerator.

Chocolate Cheesecake Bon Bons

Bite-size balls of cheesecake coated in chocolate? Um, yes. To make these dairy-free, use soy cream cheese and coconut milk.

MAKES ABOUT 30 BON BONS.

Ingredients

1 package cream cheese, softened	1 cup confectioners' sugar
2 tablespoons milk	8 ounces chocolate, chopped
1½ teaspoons vanilla extract	

Directions

1. Line a baking sheet with parchment paper.
2. Beat cream cheese, milk, and vanilla until fluffy. Gradually add confectioners' sugar, beating until combined.
3. Form dough into 1" balls and place on the lined baking sheet. Refrigerate for about 30 minutes.
4. Melt chocolate in a double boiler. Dip each ball in the melted chocolate and return to the lined baking sheet. Refrigerate for another 30 minutes before serving. Store in the refrigerator.

Peppermint Patties

I didn't even know I liked peppermint patties until I tried these. The intense peppermint flavor encased in crisp chocolate is delightful!

Makes about 24 patties.

Ingredients

14 ounces sweetened condensed milk	5 cups confectioners' sugar
1 tablespoon peppermint extract	6 cups (about 24 ounces) chocolate chips

Directions

1. Line a baking sheet with parchment paper.
2. In a medium mixing bowl, combine condensed milk and peppermint extract. Gradually add the confectioners' sugar while beating.
3. Drop dough by teaspoonfuls onto the parchment paper–lined baking sheet. Press each one down to form flat circles. Place pan in freezer for at least 10 minutes.
4. Melt the chocolate chips in the double boiler. Dip each peppermint patty and return to the baking sheet. Place baking sheet in the refrigerator until chocolate hardens. Store in the refrigerator.

Coconut Oil Peppermint Patties

Sweet, refreshing, flavorful, and basically healthy! And yes, dairy-free, too. What more need I say?

Ingredients

1 cup coconut oil	¼ teaspoon salt
½ cup honey	3 cups (about 12 ounces) chocolate
1 teaspoon peppermint oil	chips
1 teaspoon vanilla extract	

Directions

1. Stir or beat together the coconut oil, honey, peppermint oil, vanilla extract, and salt until smooth and creamy.

2. Drop dough by teaspoonfuls onto a parchment paper–lined baking sheet. Press each one down to form flat circle. Place pan in freezer for at least 10 minutes.

3. Melt or temper the chocolate chips in the double boiler. Dip each peppermint patty and return to the baking sheet. Place baking sheet in the refrigerator until chocolate hardens. Store in the refrigerator.

Orange Creams

Citrus and chocolate make such a sophisticated pair. I recommend dark chocolate for these rich beauties. To make these dairy-free and vegan, use coconut sweetened condsned milk (page xiv).

MAKES ABOUT 24 CANDIES.

Ingredients

14 ounces sweetened condensed milk

1 tablespoon orange juice

½ teaspoon orange extract

1 teaspoon orange rind, finely chopped

6 cups confectioners' sugar

24 ounces dark chocolate, finely chopped

Directions

1. Line a baking sheet with parchment paper.
2. In a medium mixing bowl, combine condensed milk, orange juice, orange extract, and orange rind. Gradually add the confectioners' sugar while beating.
3. Drop dough by teaspoonfuls onto the parchment paper–lined baking sheet. Press each one down to form flat circle. Place pan in freezer for at least 10 minutes.
4. Melt the chocolate chips in the double boiler. Dip each orange patty and return to the baking sheet. Place baking sheet in the refrigerator until chocolate hardens.

Penuchi

Penuchi is sort of a cross between fudge and caramel. I made a batch recently with coconut oil and coconut cream instead of butter and milk. It turned out a little gooier than I wanted (probably because I didn't allow it to cool enough and then didn't whip it enough before pouring it into the pan). So I rolled the mixture into little balls and wrapped each one in waxed paper. They were delicious!

MAKES ABOUT 16 PIECES.

Ingredients

2 tablespoons butter

2½ cups brown sugar

1 teaspoon vanilla

⅔ cup half-and-half or milk

½ cup chopped nuts (optional)

Directions

1. Line an 8" × 8" pan with parchment paper.
2. In a medium saucepan over low heat, stir together the butter, sugar, and cream until the mixture is melted and begins to bubble. Stop stirring and insert candy thermometer.
3. When the mixture reaches 238°F (soft ball stage), remove from heat and allow to cool to around 110°F. Add the vanilla and whip mixture until it becomes smooth and creamy.
4. Add nuts (if using) and mix. Pour into the prepared pan and refrigerate until set. Cut in 1" squares. Keep in an airtight container for a few weeks or refrigerate for longer storage.

Chocolate Caramel Peanut Butter Candy Bars

These candy bars are time-consuming, but delicious! I like to use brown rice syrup for the marshmallow-caramel layer because it's a bit healthier and it lends a nice flavor and rich brown color to the mixture, but corn syrup will also work well.

MAKES ABOUT 32 BARS.

Ingredients

Chocolate layer

1½ cups semisweet chocolate chips   ½ cup creamy peanut butter

Peanut Butter Layer

1 cup peanut butter   3 tablespoons cream cheese

1 cup confectioners' sugar

Marshmallow-Caramel Layer

3 egg whites   1 teaspoon vanilla

1 cup brown rice syrup   3 cups confectioners' sugar

¼ cup butter   1 cup peanuts, crushed

¼ cup brown sugar

Chocolate Layer

1½ cups semisweet chocolate chips   ½ cup creamy peanut butter

---

Directions

1. Grease the bottom and sides of a 9" × 13" pan.
2. Chocolate layer: In a medium saucepan over low heat, combine the chocolate chips and ½ cup peanut butter, stirring until melted and smooth. Pour into the greased pan and spread evenly. Place pan in freezer while you prepare the next layer.

Continued on next page.

3.   Peanut butter layer: Beat together the peanut butter, confectioners' sugar, and cream cheese. Spread mixture over the chocolate layer. Return to freezer.

4.   Marshmallow-Caramel Layer: Beat the egg whites until stiff. In a medium saucepan, combine brown rice syrup, butter, and brown sugar. Stir and heat until mixture reaches about 240°F (soft ball stage). Add vanilla and stir.

5.   Pour syrup mixture in a thin stream into the egg white mixture while beating. Gradually add the confectioners' sugar and beat until fully mixed.

6.   Pour mixture over the peanut butter layer and spread with a spatula. Sprinkle crushed peanuts evenly over the top.

7.   Chocolate Layer: Repeat step 2 to melt the chocolate and peanut butter, and pour mixture over the top, again spreading with a clean rubber spatula.

8.   Return to freezer or refrigerator until set. Cut in small squares to serve.

{ Taffy, Toffee, and Caramels }

Salted Caramels   34

Coconut Milk Caramels   38

Pecan Toffee   40

Salt Water Taffy   41

Caramel Corn   44

Spiced Caramel Corn   46

Peanut Butter Caramel Corn   47

Salted Caramels

Sweet, salty, and rich, homemade caramels are a chewy treat. Individually wrapped in parchment paper, they make perfect trick-or-treat candies. They can also be dipped partially or fully in melted chocolate.

MAKES ABOUT 40 PIECES.

Ingredients

1⅓ cups heavy whipping cream	½ cup dark brown sugar
5 tablespoons unsalted butter, cut into 1" pieces	¼ cup corn syrup
	¼ cup water
2 teaspoons sea salt	1 teaspoon vanilla
1½ cups granulated sugar	

Directions

1. Line an 8" × 8" pan with parchment paper. Lightly brush with oil or coat with cooking spray.
2. In a medium saucepan, combine butter, heavy cream, and 1 teaspoon salt. Stir over medium heat until melted and combined. Remove from heat and set aside.
3. In a separate medium saucepan, combine granulated sugar, dark brown sugar, corn syrup, and water. Mix over medium heat until mixture begins to boil. Insert candy thermometer and stop stirring when mixture reaches 250°F.
4. Turn off the heat and slowly pour the cream mixture into the sugar mixture, whisking until foamy and fully mixed. Turn on the heat again and allow mixture to heat to 260°F.

Continued on page 36.

When caramel is completely cooled, flip
the block of caramel over onto a board
and sprinkle with salt.

5. Remove from heat and whisk in the vanilla. Pour into the prepared pan and allow to cool for about 30 minutes. Sprinkle the remaining 1 teaspoon salt over the top.

6. When caramel is completely cool, lift the parchment paper out of the pan and peel away from the caramel. Use a sharp knife to cut the caramel into small squares. Wrap individually in waxed paper.

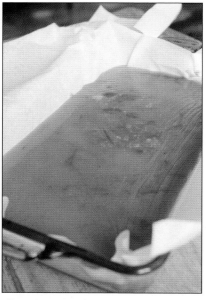

Allow the parchment paper to hang over the edges of the pan so that you can easily lift out the caramel once it's cool.

Slice the caramel into strips and then into squares. Running the knife under hot water first will make it easier to slice through the block.

Coconut Milk Caramels

These caramels are chewy and have a delicate coconut flavor. For a healthier version, you can replace the sugar and corn syrup for 1½ cups honey, maple syrup, or a combination of the two.

MAKES 64 CARAMELS.

Ingredients

1 14-ounce can coconut milk	2 cups granulated sugar
3 tablespoons coconut oil	¾ cup light corn syrup
½ teaspoon coarse salt	1 teaspoon vanilla extract or
½ cup water	coconut extract

Directions

1. Line an 8" × 8" baking dish with parchment paper, making sure the paper comes up the sides of the pan. Brush lightly with coconut oil.

2. In a medium saucepan over medium heat, combine the coconut milk, coconut oil, corn syrup, and salt. Stir occasionally until mixture is smooth, about 3 minutes.

3. In a large saucepan, combine the sugar and water over medium heat. Insert candy thermometer and heat, without stirring, to 300°F (about 10 minutes). Remove from heat and carefully pour sugar mixture into the coconut milk mixture (there may be some bubbling and splashing, so be cautious, especially if kids are helping).

4. Turn heat to low and stir gently until mixture is dissolved. Add vanilla or coconut extract, raise heat, insert candy thermometer, and keep stirring until mixture reaches 240°F. Remove from heat and pour into prepared pan.

5. Allow to cool and then invert onto a cutting board and cut into 1" squares using a knife greased with coconut oil. Wrap squares in wax paper and store at room temperature.

Pecan Toffee

Crunchy, buttery toffee is perfect sprinkled with crushed pecans and chocolate bits. If you prefer walnuts, peanuts, or a mixture, don't let anyone stop you from experimenting!

MAKES ABOUT 1 3/4 POUNDS.

Ingredients

2 cups pecans, chopped	½ teaspoon salt
1 cup sugar	¼ cup water
1 cup butter, cut into tablespoons	6 ounces chocolate, finely chopped

Directions

1. Line a baking sheet with aluminum foil and lightly grease the foil with oil. Spread 1½ cups pecan pieces evenly over the foil.

2. Combine sugar, butter, water, and salt in a medium saucepan and cook over medium heat, stirring regularly. When mixture begins to boil, insert candy thermometer.

3. When mixture reaches 300°F (hard crack stage), pour over the pecan pieces. Sprinkle remaining ½ cup pecan pieces and chocolate pieces over the top. Allow to cool and then break into pieces.

Salt Water Taffy

Traditionally made with ocean water, salt water taffy was popularized in Atlantic City in the early 1900s. Taffy requires more time and more muscle than most of the candies in this book. Be sure to start pulling the taffy before it gets too stiff (there's not a huge window of time between when it's too hot to handle and too hard to pull, especially if you've accidentally overheated your mixture). If you wait too long, you can place the taffy in a 200°F oven for a few minutes until it softens up.

MAKES A LITTLE MORE THAN A POUND OF TAFFY.

Ingredients

2 cups sugar	1 teaspoon salt
1½ tablespoons cornstarch	Few drops food coloring (optional)
1 cup light corn syrup	1 teaspoon flavoring (vanilla,
¾ cup water	lemon, mint, etc.)
2 tablespoons butter	

Directions

1. Grease an 8" × 8" baking pan.
2. In a medium saucepan, combine sugar, cornstarch, corn syrup, water, butter, and salt and stir until mixture begins to bubble. Insert candy thermometer and stop stirring when mixture reaches 250°F.
3. Remove from heat and add flavoring and food coloring. Pour onto the greased pan.
4. When mixture is cool enough to handle, grease hands with butter or oil, pick up the mixture in both hands and begin to stretch and pull it, forming a long string. Take the two ends, bring them

Continued on page 43.

together, and allow the dough to twist up. Then stretch again and repeat until the mixture lightens in color and gets a glossy sheen. This should take about 10 minutes.

5. Pull the dough into a rope that's about ½" thick. Grease scissors and cut into small pieces. Allow to sit out for about half an hour and then wrap individually in waxed paper.

Pulling taffy is a good arm workout!

Caramel Corn

To add variety to this basic recipe, add peanuts, slivered toasted almonds, dried cranberries, or drizzle with melted chocolate. To make this recipe dairy-free and vegan, use coconut oil instead of butter.

MAKES 20 CUPS.

Ingredients

6 quarts popped popcorn (1 cup unpopped)	1 cup water
	1 teaspoon salt
1 cup butter	1 teaspoon baking soda
2 cups packed brown sugar	2 teaspoons vanilla

Directions

1. Preheat oven to 250°F. Grease a large baking sheet with a lip.
2. Pour popcorn onto the baking sheet.
3. In a medium saucepan over medium heat, melt butter. Add brown sugar, water, and salt. When the mixture begins to bubble, set a timer and boil for 5 minutes without stirring.
4. Remove from heat, add baking soda and vanilla, and stir until the mixture foams. Pour the mixture over the popcorn in a thin stream, stirring with a wooden spoon to coat.
5. Bake for 1 hour, stirring every 15 minutes. Store up to a month in an airtight container.

Spiced Caramel Corn

Unique and festive, this is the perfect caramel corn recipe for the holiday season! To make this recipe dairy-free and vegan, use coconut oil instead of butter.

MAKES 20 CUPS.

Ingredients

6 quarts popped popcorn (1 cup unpopped)
1 cup cashew pieces
1 cup dried cranberries
1 cup butter
2 cups packed brown sugar
½ cup light corn syrup or brown rice syrup

1 teaspoon salt
½ teaspoon baking soda
½ teaspoon cinnamon
½ teaspoon ground ginger
1 teaspoon vanilla

Directions

1. Preheat oven to 250°F. Grease a large baking sheet with a lip.
2. Pour popcorn onto the baking sheet. Add cashew pieces and dried cranberries and stir to disperse throughout popcorn.
3. In a medium saucepan over medium heat, melt butter. Add brown sugar and corn syrup or brown rice syrup. When the mixture begins to bubble, set a timer and boil for 5 minutes without stirring. Meanwhile, combine salt, baking soda, cinnamon, and ginger in a small bowl.
4. Remove saucepan from heat, add baking soda mixture and vanilla and stir until the mixture foams. Pour the mixture over the popcorn in a thin stream, stirring with a wooden spoon to coat.
5. Bake for 1 hour, stirring every 15 minutes. Store up to a month in an airtight container.

Peanut Butter Caramel Corn

This makes a wonderful gift for peanut butter lovers. Package in a fancy tin and place a bow on top. Voila! Thoughtful and delicious gift. To make this recipe dairy-free and vegan, use coconut oil instead of butter.

MAKES 20 CUPS.

Ingredients

6 quarts popped popcorn (1 cup unpopped)
1 cup sliced almonds
1 cup butter
2 cups packed brown sugar

½ cup light corn syrup or brown rice syrup
1 teaspoon salt
½ teaspoon baking soda
1 teaspoon vanilla
1 cup smooth peanut butter

Directions

1. Preheat oven to 250°F. Grease a large baking sheet with a lip.
2. Pour popcorn onto the baking sheet.
3. In a medium saucepan over medium heat, melt butter. Add brown sugar, corn syrup or brown rice syrup, and salt. When the mixture begins to bubble, set a timer and boil for 5 minutes without stirring.
4. Remove from heat, add baking soda, vanilla, and peanut butter, and stir until the mixture foams. Pour the mixture over the popcorn in a thin stream, stirring with a wooden spoon to coat.
5. Bake for 1 hour, stirring every 15 minutes. Store up to a month in an airtight container.

{ Hard Candies, Brittles, and Bark }

Cinnamon Hard Candies	50
Citrus Hard Candy	53
Butterscotch Candy	54
Honey Lemon Ginger Drops	55
Vinegar Candy	57
Maple Nut Brittle	58
Peppermint Candy Canes	60
Rock Candy	62

Cinnamon Hard Candies

When I was about nine years old, my dad gave me a bag of cinnamon hots for Valentine's Day. I decided I was going to savor them slowly for as long as I could. I had about one candy a day until ants came and invaded my room sometime in the middle of the summer, attracted by the sugary treasure trove on my bureau. Lesson learned: some things are meant to be enjoyed in the moment and not hung onto forever!

MAKES ABOUT 1 POUND OF CANDY.

Ingredients

2¼ cups granulated sugar

1 cup water

¾ cups light corn syrup

½ teaspoon cinnamon (cassia) oil

2 drops red food coloring

Directions

1. Line a cookie sheet with foil and coat lightly with cooking spray.
2. In a medium saucepan, combine sugar, water, and corn syrup over medium heat. Stir with a metal spoon until sugar dissolves.
3. Stop stirring and insert the candy thermometer. Don't stir the syrup again until it's removed from the heat. Allow mixture to come to a boil. If sugar crystals form on the sides of the pan, wipe them away with a damp pastry brush.
4. When the syrup reaches 260°F, add the food coloring. At 300°F, remove from heat. If you're not using a candy thermometer, this is hard crack stage. Allow mixture to cool slightly until boiling has ceased. Keeping your face away from the steam rising from the syrup, add the cinnamon oil and stir. (Note: cinnamon oil is very strong and can burn your nostrils and eyes if you get your face too close to the steam.)

5. Pour the syrup onto the lined cookie sheet and use the back of a metal spoon to spread into a rectangle. Use a knife to score the candy into 1" squares. Allow to cool completely. When the candy is hard, use a sharp knife or scissors to cut the candy along the score lines.

Citrus Hard Candy

If you've made candied orange peels (page 94), reserve the liquid and then follow the recipe below starting with step 3, except that you won't need to add food coloring or fruit juice, since the syrup will already be citrusy and yellow. To make lollipops, place the lollipop sticks on your lined cookie sheet and drop spoonfuls of the syrup over one end of each stick.

MAKES ABOUT 1 POUND OF CANDY.

Ingredients

2¼ cups granulated sugar	3 teaspoons orange juice
1 cup water	2 drops yellow food coloring
¾ cup light corn syrup	(optional)

Directions

1. Line a cookie sheet with foil and coat lightly with cooking spray.
2. In a medium saucepan, combine sugar, water, and corn syrup over medium heat. Stir with a metal spoon until sugar dissolves.
3. Stop stirring and insert the candy thermometer. Don't stir the syrup again until it's removed from the heat. Allow mixture to come to a boil. If sugar crystals form on the sides of the pan, wipe them away with a damp pastry brush.
4. When the syrup reaches 260°F, add the food coloring. At 300°F, remove from heat. If you're not using a candy thermometer, this is hard crack stage. Allow mixture to cool slightly until boiling has ceased. Add the fruit juice and stir.
5. Pour the syrup onto the lined cookie sheet and use the back of a metal spoon to spread into a rectangle. Use a knife to score the candy into 1" squares. Allow to cool completely. When the candy is hard, use a sharp knife or scissors to cut the candy along the score lines.

Butterscotch Candy

Traditionally these buttery candies are hard, but melt in your mouth. If you prefer them a little chewy, add all the ingredients except the rum or vanilla extract at the beginning and remove from heat at 255°F. Continue with steps 3 and 4 below.

MAKES ABOUT 1 1/2 POUNDS.

Ingredients

1 cup unsalted butter, cut into 1" pieces	½ cup corn syrup or brown rice syrup
2 cups white granulated sugar	¼ cup honey
½ cup brown sugar	½ teaspoon salt
¾ cup water	½ teaspoon rum or vanilla extract

Directions

1. Line a 9" x 13" baking pan with parchment paper and spray lightly with cooking spray.

2. In a heavy saucepan over medium heat, combine the sugars, water, and corn syrup or brown rice syrup. Stir until sugar melts, and then insert candy thermometer and heat without stirring until mixture reaches 270°F. Add the honey, salt, and butter. Stir until mixture reaches 300°F.

3. Remove from heat, stir in the rum or vanilla extract, and pour into the lined pan. Allow to cool for about 2 minutes and then use a sharp knife to score the candy in 1" squares.

4. After several minutes, once candy is fully set, use the edges of the paper to lift the candy out of the pan and turn it onto a clean surface. Peel off the paper, and break into squares. Store in an airtight container.

Honey Lemon Ginger Drops

These little candies double as throat lozenges. Made with honey rather than processed sugar and spiked with vinegar and lemon juice, they are healthier than most store-bought lozenges, and as tasty as any candy you'll try.

MAKES A LITTLE LESS THAN 1 POUND OF DROPS.

Ingredients

½ cup water
3" piece of ginger root, peeled and finely diced
1 cup honey
2 tablespoons apple cider vinegar

2 teaspoons fresh-squeezed lemon juice
½ teaspoon slippery elm powder (optional)

Directions

1. Line a cookie sheet with parchment paper and spray lightly with cooking spray.

2. In a small saucepan, simmer the water and ginger for about half an hour. Strain, reserving the liquid. (You can toss the ginger bits in sugar, let them dry on a cookie sheet, and enjoy them as chewy ginger candies.)

3. In a medium saucepan, combine the ginger water, honey, and vinegar. Stir with a metal spoon until honey liquefies.

4. Stop stirring and insert the candy thermometer. Don't stir the syrup again until it's removed from the heat. Allow mixture to come to a boil. If sugar crystals form on the sides of the pan, wipe them away with a damp pastry brush.

Continued on next page.

5. When the syrup reaches 300°F, remove from heat. If you're not using a candy thermometer, this is hard crack stage. Allow mixture to cool slightly until boiling has ceased. Add the lemon juice and stir.

6. Working quickly, use a ½ teaspoon measure to drop the syrup onto the lined cookie sheet, leaving a little space between each one. If desired, sprinkle with slippery elm powder. Let cool for at least ½ hour. Store for about a week at room temperature or refrigerate for longer storage.

Vinegar Candy

This old-fashioned recipe is simple and delicious. Who knew vinegar could be so tasty?

MAKES ABOUT 40 PIECES.

Ingredients

2 cups sugar	1 tablespoon butter
½ cup apple cider vinegar	½ teaspoon vanilla

Directions

1. Grease a baking sheet (choose one with a lip).
2. Combine sugar, vinegar, and butter in a saucepan and heat while stirring until melted and combined. Insert thermometer and heat to 270°F.
3. Remove from heat, add vanilla, and stir. Pour mixture onto the baking sheet. When cool, break into pieces. Store between layers of waxed paper in an airtight container.

Maple Nut Brittle

Nut brittles are easy to make, but have all your ingredients ready before you start because you can't waste any time between steps. If you find that your brittle isn't hardening, you can scoop it up, return it to the saucepan, and reheat it—chances are you didn't cook it quite long enough the first time.

MAKES ABOUT 2 POUNDS OF BRITTLE.

Ingredients

2 cups roasted and salted nuts (peanuts, pecans, or walnuts)	½ cup water
	1 cup maple syrup
2 cups sugar	1 teaspoon baking soda

Directions

1. Coat a rimmed cookie sheet with cooking spray.
2. In a medium saucepan, heat the sugar, water, and maple syrup. Continue at a slow boil, stirring gently, until mixture reaches 245°F. Add the nuts and stir.
3. When the mixture reaches 300°F, add the baking soda, stir, and remove from heat. Mixture will foam, so be careful.
4. Pour onto the greased pan and use a wooden spoon or spatula to spread the mixture. Cool completely before breaking into pieces.

Peppermint Candy Canes

Homemade candy canes? How cool! I recommend wearing gloves for the pulling process. If there are two of you, one can pull the white dough while the other pulls the red.

MAKES ABOUT 1 DOZEN CANDY CANES.

Ingredients

2 cups sugar	¼ teaspoon cream of tartar
½ cup light corn syrup	¾ teaspoon peppermint extract
¼ cup water	Red gel food coloring

Directions

1. Lightly coat two cookie sheets with oil or a Silipat matt. Preheat oven to 170°F.

2. In a medium saucepan, combine the sugar, corn syrup, water, and cream of tartar. Stir gently over medium heat until mixture dissolves. Insert candy thermometer, stop stirring, and heat until mixture reaches 260°F (hard ball stage).

3. Remove from heat and add peppermint extract. Pour half the mixture onto one cookie sheet and place in the oven. Add a few drops of food coloring to the remaining mixture and stir.

4. Pour red mixture onto the second cookie sheet. Allow to rest until a thin skin forms over the mixture. Lightly grease a metal spatula and use it to push and spread the dough around on the pan, helping it to cool.

5. When dough is cool enough to handle, pick it up in both hands and begin to stretch and pull it, forming a long string. Take the two ends, bring them together, and allow the dough to twist up. Then stretch again and repeat until the dough becomes opaque.

6. Before the dough hardens, form it into a rope that is about 2" thick and return the pan to the oven to stay warm.

7. Remove the white dough from the oven and repeat step 5 with it, ending with a 2" thick rope. Remove the first pan from the oven.

8. Cut equal lengths of both the red rope and the white rope. Twist them together, bend over one end to form the crook of the cane, and place on the cookie sheet to cool (you may want to re-grease the pan if the dough has absorbed the oil). Repeat until all the rope is used. Work as quickly as you can, and return pans to the oven to reheat slightly if the dough gets too hard to mold.

9. Candy canes will harden at room temperature but then will soften over time. Wrap candy canes individually in plastic wrap to keep from getting soft.

Rock Candy

If you've never made rock candy, you're missing out. It's fascinating to watch the sugar crystals form along the skewers. To make these work, your sugar to water ratio needs to be two to one. It's a good idea to cover the glasses lightly with cheesecloth to keep dust out, but don't use a heavy cloth or plastic since the mixture needs air to evaporate properly.

MAKES 2 SKEWERS.

Ingredients

2 cups water	Clothespins
4 cups granulated sugar	Tall, skinny glasses or jars, or short
Food coloring	vases (champagne flutes work
Wooden skewers with the sharp	well)
points cut off	

Directions

1. Combine the sugar and water in a medium saucepan. Over medium heat, stir until all the sugar dissolves and the syrup begins to boil.

2. Remove from heat and divide syrup between glasses. Put a few drops of food coloring in each glass and stir. You can make each one a different color, if desired.

3. Clip a clothespin onto the end of each skewer and put one skewer in each glass, making sure the skewer doesn't quite reach the bottom of the glass. Put the glasses in a safe place (where they won't get knocked over!) and allow to sit for about a week, or until the crystals are well formed along the skewers.

4. To remove the skewers from the glasses, use a knife to gently break the crystals on the surface around the skewer and then carefully pull out the skewers. Empty any remaining liquid into the sink, and then return the skewers back to the glasses to drip dry.

5. Once dry, rock candy can be wrapped in cellophane to store.

TIP

Rock candy can be made on a wooden tea stirrer and then used to sweeten coffee or tea. You can also use 3 cups of sugar and 1 cup of honey in this recipe, rather than using all sugar.

{ Soft Candies, Marshmallows, and Meringues }

Applet Candies	66
Coconut Clouds	68
Mocha Meringue Bark	70
Black Licorice Twists	71
Gummy Candies	72
Homemade Marshmallows	74
Marzipan	76
Opera Creams	77
Raspberry Pate de Fruit	78
Citrus Pate de Fruit	79
Simple Jam Pate de Fruit	80
Potato Candy	82
Divinity	83
Candy Corn	84
Sesame Halvah	88

Applet Candies

Soft and delicate, there is something especially luxurious about these little candies. Applets are similar to Turkish delight and pate de fruit, but with their own distinct flavor.

MAKES ABOUT 50 CANDIES.

Ingredients

---

2 cups unsweetened applesauce

4 packets unflavored gelatin

3 cups sugar

1 teaspoon vanilla extract

½ teaspoon lemon juice

Confectioners' sugar

½ cup chopped walnuts (if desired)

Directions

1. Grease the bottom and sides of an 8" × 8" pan.
2. In a small dish, combine ½ cup applesauce and the gelatin. Pour the remaining 1½ cups applesauce into a saucepan and bring to a boil. Add the applesauce-gelatin mixture and allow to boil slowly for 15 minutes, stirring constantly.
3. Remove from heat and add the vanilla extract, lemon juice, and walnuts.
4. Allow to sit out for 24 hours, or until applets are firm enough to cut. Slice into squares and roll in confectioners' sugar. Store in the refrigerator.

Coconut Clouds

These meringues are crisp on the outside and slightly chewy on the inside. To ensure that the egg whites whip properly, make sure that the bowl and beaters are completely dry before you start.

MAKES ABOUT 24 PIECES.

Ingredients

3 egg whites	¾ cup granulated sugar
⅛ teaspoon cream of tartar	1½ cups toasted coconut flakes

Directions

1. Preheat oven to 250°F. Line a cookie sheet with aluminum foil.
2. Beat egg whites and cream of tartar until they form soft peaks. Gradually add the sugar, and continue beating until the mixture is glossy and forms stiff peaks.
3. Gently fold in the coconut flakes and pour mixture onto the lined cookie sheet. Use a spatula to spread the mixture into a rectangle that is about ½" thick.
4. Bake for an hour, or until the meringue is dry and crisp. Allow to cool and then break into small pieces.
5. Store in an airtight container for about a week.

Mocha Meringue Bark

This bark is sweet, crisp, and perfect with a cup of coffee, hot cocoa, or eggnog.

MAKES ABOUT 12 PIECES.

Ingredients

3 egg whites

⅛ teaspoon cream of tartar

¾ cup granulated sugar

½ cup almond flour

1 tablespoon instant coffee granules

1 tablespoon cocoa powder

¼ cup mini chocolate chips

Directions

1. Preheat oven to 250°F. Line a cookie sheet with aluminum foil.
2. In a completely dry bowl, using completely dry beaters, beat egg whites and cream of tartar until they form soft peaks. Gradually add the sugar, and continue beating until the mixture is glossy and forms stiff peaks.
3. In a separate bowl, combine the almond flour, coffee granules, and cocoa powder. Gently fold mixture into the egg whites and pour batter onto the lined cookie sheet. Use a spatula to spread the mixture into a rectangle that is about ¼" thick. Sprinkle with mini chocolate chips.
4. Bake for about an hour, or until the meringue is dry and crisp. Allow to cool and then break into small pieces.
5. Store in an airtight container for about a week.

Black Licorice Twists

If you're a licorice lover, you must try this recipe! If you don't find anise extract at your local grocery store, check out the resource section on page 111.

MAKES ABOUT 36 TWISTS.

Ingredients

1 cup salted butter, divided into tablespoons

1 cup granulated sugar

½ cup corn syrup

¼ cup molasses

½ cup sweetened condensed milk

¾ cup whole wheat or all-purpose flour

2 teaspoons anise extract or oil of licorice root

1 teaspoon black food coloring

Directions

1. Line an 8" × 8" pan with foil and coat lightly with cooking spray.
2. In a medium saucepan, combine the sugar, corn syrup, and molasses and stir over medium heat. Add the butter and stir until melted. Insert a candy thermometer.
3. When the mixture reaches 260°F (hard ball stage), remove from heat and stir in the flour, extract or oil, and coloring.
4. Pour mixture into the foil-lined pan and chill for about half an hour.
5. Lift foil from pan or invert pan onto a cutting board. Cut the licorice into ¼" thick strips and twist. Chill for another half hour.

Gummy Candies

These gooey candies are a bit messy to make, but the kids will love them! Wear gloves if you don't want your fingers stained pretty colors.

MAKES ABOUT 60 CANDIES.

Ingredients

4 cups white sugar	4 envelopes knox gelatin
1½ cups cold water	Flavoring extracts
1½ cups boiling water	Food coloring

Directions

1. Coat four shallow 8" × 8" baking pans with cooking spray.
2. In a medium saucepan, combine the gelatin and cold water, stir gently, and allow to sit for 5 minutes.
3. Add the boiling water and sugar and stir. Over medium–high heat, boil the mixture for about 25 minutes while stirring.
4. Remove from heat and divide between four bowls. Add a couple drops of extract and a couple drops of coloring to each bowl and stir.
5. Pour each into one of the pans and refrigerate overnight.
6. When gum drops are mostly firm, slice into small squares or use your fingers to form the candies into desired shapes. Roll in sugar and place on a parchment paper–lined cookie sheet to set for 2 days.

Homemade Marshmallows

Serve homemade marshmallows with a cup of steaming hot chocolate, in s'mores, or all on their own for a really special treat.

MAKES ABOUT 24 2½ INCH MARSHMALLOWS.

Ingredients

1 cup cold water	¾ cup light corn syrup
3 envelopes (3 tablespoons)	¼ teaspoon salt
unflavored gelatin	1 teaspoon vanilla
2 cups sugar	Confectioners' sugar

Directions

1. Line a 9" × 13" × 2" pan with parchment paper and dust the paper with about 3 tablespoons of confectioners' sugar.

2. Pour ½ cup cold water in a bowl, sprinkle the gelatin over the water, and let rest for about 15 minutes.

3. Meanwhile, heat the other ½ cup water, sugar, salt, and corn syrup in a 2-quart saucepan over medium heat, stirring until the sugar dissolves and the mixture comes to a boil.

4. Cover and allow to boil for about 3 minutes to dissolve any sugar crystals on the sides of the pan.

5. Remove the lid, turn up the heat, insert a candy thermometer, and don't stir until the temperature reaches 240°F. Remove from the heat.

6. Use an electric beater at medium speed to begin beating the gelatin and water mixture, adding the syrup in a slow, thin stream. Once added, increase the speed to high and beat for another 10 minutes. The mixture will turn white, fluffy, and sticky. Add the vanilla and beat another minute or so to combine.

7. Scoop the marshmallow fluff into the prepared pan, using a damp spatula to spread it as smoothly as possible. Dust the top with another 3 tablespoons confectioners' sugar. Set in a cool, dry place and allow to sit, uncovered, for 12 hours.

8. To remove the marshmallows from the pan, run a knife around the edges of the pan to loosen the marshmallows. Then invert the pan onto a cutting board dusted with more confectioners' sugar. Peel off the parchment paper and cut the marshmallows into squares. Store in an airtight container for up to 2 weeks.

MAKE IT VEGAN!

Gelatin is often derived from animal products. You can substitute the gelatin for 3 tablespoons powdered agar-agar, or look for a kosher gelatin, which is more likely to be vegan.

Marzipan

Marzipan is wonderfully versatile. You can mold it into any shape you like, use it to decorate cakes, or roll it into balls and dip it in chocolate.

MAKES ABOUT 2 CUPS.

Ingredients

3 cups whole blanched almonds	2 egg whites, lightly beaten (or
2¼ cups confectioners' sugar,	liquid pasteurized egg whites)
divided	½ teaspoon almond extract

Directions

1. In a food processor, pulverize the almonds with the confectioners' sugar. When the nuts are finely ground (but before they turn into almond butter), add the egg whites and almond extract and continue to process until the dough clumps together into a ball.

2. Turn the dough onto a board dusted with confectioners' sugar and knead until smooth. Use immediately or wrap in plastic and store in the refrigerator for up to 3 months.

3. Allow dough to warm to room temperature before use. Roll the dough into your favorite shapes and serve.

Opera Creams

Smooth and delicious, opera creams can be enjoyed as they are or dipped in your favorite chocolate.

MAKES ABOUT 20 CREAMS.

Ingredients

2 cups sugar	⅛ teaspoon salt
2 tablespoons light corn syrup	1 teaspoon vanilla extract
1 cup whipping cream	1 cup toasted sliced almonds or
4 tablespoons unsalted butter	pecans

Directions

1. Combine all ingredients except for vanilla and nuts in a medium saucepan. Stir until combined, bring to a slow boil, and insert candy thermometer. Don't stir again, allowing the mixture to reach 238°F (soft ball stage).

2. Remove from heat and allow to cool to 110°F. Add vanilla and nuts and whisk until mixture becomes thick. Drop small spoonfuls onto a cookie sheet lined with parchment paper. Allow to rest until cool and set.

Raspberry Pate de Fruit

This is the perfect treat to make with raspberries that are just a little too ripe. Sweet and summery, these are as pretty as they are delicious.

Ingredients

1½ pounds (about 3 cups) fresh or thawed raspberries

2 cups granulated sugar, plus more for dusting

1 tablespoon powdered pectin

½ teaspoon lemon juice

Directions

1. Line an 8" × 8" pan with parchment paper, making sure the paper hangs over the edges of the pan a bit.

2. Cook the raspberries in a medium saucepan over low heat for about 10 minutes, stirring gently. When the raspberries are soft and mushy, strain them through a fine sieve to remove the seeds.

3. Return the raspberry purée to the saucepan and add the sugar and pectin. Insert your candy thermometer and heat the mixture to 220°F. Remove from heat and stir in the lemon juice.

4. Pour the mixture into the paper-lined pan and refrigerate for 3–4 hours.

5. When the candy is set, dust a wooden cutting board with sugar. Invert the pan onto the cutting board and remove the parchment paper. Run a sharp knife under hot water and then slice the candy into squares. Roll in additional sugar.

6. Store in a covered container at room temperature for up to 2 weeks, or longer in the refrigerator.

Citrus Pate de Fruit

For a beautiful candy display, make three batches, each with a different citrus flavor and color, and serve together.

MAKES ABOUT 30 PIECES.

Ingredients

⅔ cup orange, lemon, lime, or grapefruit juice (or a combination)

1½ cups unsweetened, smooth applesauce

1 tablespoon powdered pectin

2½ cups granulated sugar, plus more for dusting

½ teaspoon zest (from lemon, lime, or grapefruit)

Few drops food coloring (optional)

Directions

1. Line an 8" × 8" pan with parchment paper, making sure the paper hangs over the edges of the pan a bit.

2. In a medium saucepan over medium heat, combine the citrus juice, applesauce, pectin, and 1 cup sugar. Clip a thermometer to your pan and stir mixture gently. When mixture begins to bubble, add another 1 cup of sugar.

3. When mixture reaches 220°F, remove from heat and stir in the citrus zest and food coloring, if using.

4. Pour the mixture into the paper-lined pan and refrigerate for 3–4 hours.

5. When the candy is set, dust a wooden cutting board with sugar. Invert the pan onto the cutting board and remove the parchment paper. Run a sharp knife under hot water and then slice the candy into squares. Roll in additional sugar. Store in a covered container at room temperature for up to 2 weeks, or longer in the refrigerator.

Simple Jam Pate de Fruit

These delightful candies can be made with any kind of jam. Blueberry jam was used in the candies shown here.

MAKES ABOUT 30 PIECES.

Ingredients

⅔ cup applesauce

⅓ cup water

2 envelopes gelatin

¾ cup sugar

1 cup jam

1 teaspoon lemon juice

Directions

1. Combine ⅓ cup applesauce, water, and gelatin, and let sit for about 5 minutes. Lightly oil an 8" × 8" baking pan.
2. In a medium saucepan, combine other ⅓ cup applesauce and sugar, stirring until it begins to boil. Add the jam and mix until fully melted and combined. Add the gelatin mixture and lemon juice and stir. Allow to boil for 2–3 minutes.
3. Pour into the prepared pan and refrigerate at least 4 hours.
4. Wet a sharp knife to cut the candies into squares. Use a small spatula to carefully remove the squares from the pan. Coat each square with sugar. Store at room temperature in an airtight container between layers of waxed paper for up to 3 weeks.

MAKE IT VEGAN!

Gelatin is often derived from animal products. You can substitute 2 tablespoons plus 2 teaspoons powdered agar-agar, or look for a kosher gelatin, which is more likely to be vegan.

Potato Candy

These pinwheel candies are the perfect use for leftover mashed potatoes! To make these dairy-free, use coconut milk instead of cow's milk and peanut butter instead of Nutella.

MAKES 48 PIECES.

Ingredients

1 medium potato	2 pounds confectioners' sugar
1 teaspoon milk	2 cups peanut butter or Nutella (or a
1 teaspoon vanilla	mix of the two)

Directions

1. Peel, chop, and boil potato until soft (test by poking the potato with a fork—if it goes in easily, it's done). Drain the potato and mash it together with the milk and vanilla. Add the confectioners' sugar gradually, mixing and mashing until dough is stiff enough to form a ball. Add more confectioners' sugar if dough is too goopy.

2. Spread parchment paper on a work surface and dust with more confectioners' sugar. Roll out the dough to about ½" thick. Dust with more sugar, then spread peanut butter or Nutella evenly over the surface.

3. Roll the dough into one long log (like a jelly roll) and refrigerate for about an hour (you can cut the log into two pieces so it will fit better in your fridge).

4. Once chilled, slice the log into ½" pieces and serve.

Divinity

These candies will melt in your mouth (okay, so that's technically true of most candies, but you'll really notice it with these—in the most wonderful way). Beware that these may not stiffen properly if the air is particularly humid—it's best to make these on a relatively dry day.

MAKES ABOUT 4 DOZEN.

Ingredients

2 cups sugar

½ cup light corn syrup

¾ cup water

1 teaspoon vanilla

½ teaspoon salt

3 egg whites

¾ cup nuts, chopped

Directions

1. Combine sugar, corn syrup, and water in a medium saucepan. Stir over medium heat until sugar is dissolved. Increase heat and bring to a boil. Cover and boil without stirring 3 minutes.

2. Uncover, insert candy thermometer, and cook until syrup reaches 260°F (firm ball stage). Remove from heat.

3. In a separate bowl, beat egg whites until stiff peaks form. Add salt and vanilla. With mixer at high speed, beat in hot syrup, slowly pouring in a thin stream.

4. Continue beating until mixture will almost hold its shape but is still glossy. Stir in nuts if desired. Drop by spoonfuls onto parchment paper.

Candy Corn

Candy corn is great to make with kids. Rolling out the dough is a lot like playing with playdough!

MAKES ABOUT 3 CUPS.

Ingredients

---

1 cup granulated sugar

⅔ cup light corn syrup

5 tablespoons butter, cut into pieces

2 teaspoons vanilla

3 cups confectioners' sugar

⅓ cup powdered milk

¼ teaspoon salt

Yellow and orange food coloring

MAKE IT VEGAN!

Use vegan margarine instead of butter and use powdered soy milk.

Directions

1. In a medium saucepan over low heat, stir together granulated sugar, corn syrup, and butter. Once melted and combined, increase heat and allow to boil for about 5 minutes. Remove from heat and stir in vanilla.

2. In a large mixing bowl, stir together the confectioners' sugar, powdered milk, and salt. Pour the syrup mixture into the dry mixture and combine.

3. Prepare a large wooden cutting board or other surface by dusting with confectioners' sugar. When dough is cool enough to handle, divide evenly into three pieces. Put a couple drops of yellow food coloring on one piece and a couple drops of orange food coloring on the second piece. Leave the third piece white.

Continued on next page.

4. Coat hands with more confectioners' sugar and begin to knead each piece until the colors are incorporated and dough is smooth and stiff. Then roll out each piece between your palms like you're making playdough snakes. Place the pieces together and press down gently. If they're not sticking together well, brush the edges lightly with water and try again.

5. Cut into triangles and allow to air dry for a couple of hours before storing in a bag or airtight container.

Step 4: Roll the dough into thin snakes, place together, and press down gently.

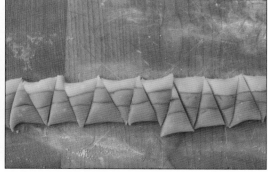

Step 5: Cut into triangles to form the corn-shaped pieces.

Sesame Halvah

I'm one quarter Jewish, which, as far as I'm concerned, is enough to justify indulging in really good halvah on a fairly regular basis. Fortunately, this halvah recipe is actually relatively healthy, and can be used in a variety of ways—crumbled and used with frosting or Nutella as a cake filling; dipped in chocolate to make an amazing candy bar; crushed and dusted over ice cream; or just all on its own.

MAKES ABOUT 2 POUNDS.

Ingredients

2 cups honey	1½ cups nuts (almonds, pistachios,
1½ cups tahini	or hazelnuts), peeled and lightly
1 teaspoon vanilla	toasted

Directions

1. Lightly grease a 6-cup mold or cake pan.
2. Beat or stir the tahini to incorporate the oil into the sesame paste.
3. In a medium saucepan over low heat, bring the honey to a simmer. Insert candy thermometer and heat to 240°F (soft ball stage). Remove from heat and allow to cool to 120°F. Add the vanilla and nuts and then the tahini and stir gently.
4. Pour into the greased pan, cover with plastic, and refrigerate for 24 to 36 hours.

{ Fruits, Nuts, and Other Sweetmeats }

Crystallized Ginger   92

Fruit Leather   93

Candied Orange Peels   94

Candy-Coated Nuts   96

Caramelized Mixed Nuts   97

Chocolate-Dipped Fruit Skewers   98

Pecan Pralines   99

Dates Stuffed with Goat Cheese and Chocolate   100

Raisin Clusters   102

Dried Cherry and Chocolate Balls   103

Sugar Plums   104

Apricot-Orange Balls   106

Brandy Balls   107

Walnut Clusters   108

Crystallized Ginger

Zingy and slightly chewy, crystallized ginger can help to alleviate nausea and generally aid digestion. Reserve the liquid from the recipe for use in Honey Lemon Ginger Drops (page 55) or for use in homemade ginger ale!

MAKES 1 POUND.

Ingredients

1 pound fresh ginger root, peeled and sliced ⅛" thick	4 cups granulated sugar
	4 cups water

Directions

1. Place the peeled and sliced ginger in a saucepan with the water and sugar, stir, and simmer over medium–high heat for about half an hour.
2. With a slotted spoon, scoop out the ginger and place on a wire rack. Allow to dry and then toss ginger in granulated sugar.
3. Store in an airtight container.

Fruit Leather

If you have a food dehydrator, use that instead of your oven for this recipe! If you decide to use raspberries, strawberries, or any fruit that contains small seeds, push purée through a strainer to remove seeds before baking. Experiment with adding a dash of cinnamon, ginger, orange zest, or other spices or flavorings.

MAKES 6 TO 8 SERVINGS.

Ingredients

3 cups applesauce or other puréed fruit	2 tablespoons honey ⅛ teaspoon salt

Directions

1. Line a rimmed baking sheet with parchment paper or a silicone baking mat. Heat oven to 170°F.
2. Mix ingredients together and then pour onto the lined baking sheet. Spread evenly with a rubber spatula. Bake for 6 to 7 hours.
3. When the fruit mixture is sufficiently leathery, remove from oven and allow to cool. Remove paper and cut into shapes or strips.
4. Store between layers of parchment paper up to 3 weeks.

Candied Orange Peels

These candies are simple to make and will fill your kitchen with a delightful citrus scent while they cook. If desired, dip the tips of the finished candied peels in melted chocolate and allow to set for an hour or so before serving. The cooking syrup can be retained and used as a citrusy simple syrup to mix into iced tea or used to make lollipops or other hard candy (see page 53).

MAKES ABOUT 1 CUP OF CANDY.

Ingredients

3 oranges (peels only)   3 cups water
5 cups sugar, divided

Directions

1. In a large saucepan, bring 3 cups of water to a boil. Wash the orange peels and slice them into strips ¼" wide. Place in the boiling water and cook for 15 minutes. Drain into a colander and rinse the peels.

2. In the saucepan whisk together 3 cups of water with 4 cups of sugar. Bring to a boil over medium heat. Add the peels and simmer over low heat for about 45 minutes.

3. Drain into a colander, reserving the syrup for other uses.

4. Place 1 cup of sugar in a bowl and toss the peels until well coated. Transfer peels to a baking sheet lined with aluminum foil. Let stand for 1 to 2 days or until coating is dried. Extras can be stored in the freezer for up to 2 months.

Candy-Coated Nuts

These are the perfect party treat. Place them in a bowl next to the drinks for people to nibble on as they mingle.

MAKES 4 CUPS.

Ingredients

2 egg whites	1 teaspoon cinnamon
½ cup granulated sugar	½ teaspoon salt
½ cup brown sugar	4 cups raw pecan halves, peanuts, or
1 teaspoon vanilla	cashews

Directions

1. Preheat oven to 275°F. Grease a cookie sheet.
2. Beat egg whites until stiff, add granulated sugar, brown sugar, vanilla, cinnamon, and salt and continue to beat for about a minute.
3. Combine mixture with nuts and toss to coat the nuts. Spread the nuts on the greased cookie sheet and bake for about 45 minutes, stirring every 15 minutes. Remove from oven and cool.

Caramelized Mixed Nuts

Similar to the sweet nuts you can buy from the carts in New York City, these are easy to make and sure to please any nut-loving crowd.

MAKES 2 CUPS.

Ingredients

2 cups mixed nuts (blanched almonds, unsalted roasted cashews, pecan halves, walnut halves)	½ cup light brown sugar ¼ cup water 1½ tablespoons honey 2 tablespoons butter

Directions

1. In a medium saucepan, combine the sugar, water, and honey and bring to a boil. Add the butter and stir until melted. Add the nuts and stir.

2. Boil for about two minutes and then stir vigorously. When the water evaporates, turn off the heat and continue stirring as the sugar caramelizes on the nuts. Pour the nuts onto a baking sheet lined with parchment paper to cool.

Chocolate-Dipped Fruit Skewers

Chocolate-dipped fruit lends an elegant touch to any gathering. You can use fresh or dried fruit for this recipe (no need to wash dried fruit before dipping).

MAKES 1 POUND.

Ingredients

6 ounces semisweet or dark chocolate, chopped
1 pound berries, pineapple, bananas, dried apricots, or any other fruit

⅛ to ¼ teaspoon spices (optional) such as cinnamon, cayenne, cardamom, or ginger
Toppings (optional) such as coarse sugar, cacao nibs, sprinkles, or crushed nuts
Wooden skewers

Directions

1. Wash fruit and pat dry. Berries can stay whole, but larger fruit should be chopped into bite-size pieces.
2. Melt chocolate in a double boiler. Add spice, if using, and stir with spatula. Keep heat on low.
3. Pierce each piece of fruit with a skewer and dip in the chocolate. Roll the fruit in your desired topping and place on a cookie sheet lined with parchment paper. Chocolate will set within a few minutes. Extras can be stored in the refrigerator.

Pecan Pralines

To make these sweet treats extra special, add 1 tablespoon bourbon along with the vanilla. Yum!

MAKES ABOUT 2 CUPS OF PRALINES.

Ingredients

4 tablespoons butter	½ cup heavy cream
2 cups brown sugar	2 cups pecan halves
⅛ teaspoon salt	2 teaspoons vanilla extract

Directions

1. Heat oven to 350°F. Spread pecan halves on a greased baking sheet and toast for about 4 minutes. Stir and toast for another 4 minutes. Remove from oven.

2. In a medium saucepan, melt the butter. Add brown sugar, salt, and cream. Stir over medium heat and insert a candy thermometer.

3. When mixture reaches 242°F (almost firm ball stage), remove from heat and add the vanilla and mix. Add the toasted nuts and stir vigorously until candy loses its sheen and becomes creamy.

4. Drop candy by teaspoonfuls onto the cookie sheet, working quickly. Allow to cool. To store the candy, wrap each piece individually in plastic or wax paper.

Dates Stuffed with Goat Cheese and Chocolate

Dates are naturally very sweet and are delicious paired with savory goat cheese.

MAKES 24 CANDIES.

Ingredients

24 whole pitted medjool dates

¼ cup goat cheese

2 teaspoons unsweetened cocoa powder

3 teaspoons confectioners' sugar

Directions

1. Cut a slit along the length of each date.
2. In a small bowl, mix together the goat cheese, cocoa powder, and 1 teaspoon confectioners' sugar. Place a small scoop of the mixture inside each date. Sift remaining confectioners' sugar over the tops of the dates.
3. Serve immediately or store in the refrigerator for up to a few days.

Raisin Clusters

These candies are great if you're looking for a quick, easy-to-make crowd pleaser. To make these dairy-free, use coconut sweetened condensed milk (page xiv).

MAKES ABOUT 30 CLUSTERS.

Ingredients

1 cup semisweet chocolate chips	1 teaspoon vanilla
⅓ cup sweetened condensed milk	2 cups raisins

Directions
1. Line a baking sheet with parchment paper.
2. In a double boiler, melt the chocolate chips with the sweetened condensed milk. Add vanilla and stir. Remove from heat and mix in the raisins.
3. Drop by teaspoonfuls onto the prepared baking sheet. Refrigerate for about half an hour, or until firm. Store in an airtight container, with parchment paper separating the layers of candies.

Dried Cherry and Chocolate Balls

Dried cherries are getting easier to find, which is wonderful because they are *so good*! These candies are relatively healthy and make a great afternoon pick-me-up.

MAKES ABOUT 24 BALLS.

Ingredients

1 cup dried cherries
½ cup almond butter
3 tablespoons honey
3 tablespoons coconut oil

1 cup crisp rice cereal
8 ounces bittersweet chocolate, chopped

Directions

1. Combine cherries, almond butter, honey, and coconut oil in a food processor and pulse until chopped and combined. Scoop into a large mixing bowl, add rice cereal, and mix. Roll mixture into 1" balls and set on a parchment paper–lined baking sheet. Refrigerate for about 30 minutes.

2. Melt chocolate in a double boiler. Dip each ball in the chocolate and return to the baking sheet. Refrigerate for about 30 minutes. Store in airtight container in refrigerator about 2 weeks.

Sugar Plums

Confession: I didn't even know what sugar plums were until recently. But once I tried these healthy treats, I loved them!

MAKES ABOUT 1 1/2 CUPS OF CANDY.

Ingredients

½ cup almonds, hazelnuts, or walnuts (or a mix)

¾ cup Medjool dates, prunes, dried cranberries, or raisins (or a mix)

1 tablespoon honey

3 tablespoons nut butter (almond, peanut, or cashew)

⅛ teaspoon almond extract

⅛ teaspoon vanilla

½ teaspoon cinnamon

⅛ teaspoon cloves

½ cup raw, coarse sugar

Directions

1. In a food processor, pulse together the dried fruit and nuts. Add the remaining ingredients except for the sugar and pulse until mixture starts to clump together.
2. Roll the dough into small balls and roll in the sugar. Store in an airtight container between layers of waxed paper for up to a month.

Apricot-Orange Balls

Typically a holiday treat, these easy confections can be whipped up and enjoyed any time of year. Make ahead and store in the refrigerator and then pull them out and display in a candy dish for an easy party treat.

MAKES ABOUT 24 BALLS.

Ingredients

1 cup dried apricots or peaches	3 tablespoons honey
⅔ cup lightly toasted nuts	2 teaspoons grated orange zest
(hazelnuts, walnuts, almonds, or	2 tablespoons orange juice or rum
pecans work well)	3 ounces bittersweet chocolate

Directions

1. In a food processor, pulse apricots and nuts just until finely chopped. Scoop mixture into a bowl and add honey sugar, orange zest, and orange juice. Roll mixture into 1" balls and set on a parchment paper–lined baking sheet.

2. Melt chocolate in a double boiler. Drizzle chocolate over tops of the balls in a zig-zag pattern. Refrigerate for about 30 minutes. Store in airtight container in refrigerator about 2 weeks.

Brandy Balls

To make these treats gluten-free, use gluten-free graham crackers or substitute with rice or corn cereal. Since neither rum nor brandy are grain-based, most varieties are gluten-free, but depending on how severe the gluten allergy or intolerance, you may want to double check with the manufacturer.

MAKES ABOUT 5 1/2 CUPS OF CANDY.

Ingredients

4 cups walnuts
1½ cups crushed vanilla wafers or graham crackers
½ cup rum

½ cup brandy
½ cup honey
Confectioners' sugar, for rolling

Directions

1. In a food processor, pulse the walnuts until finely ground (you may need to do 1 cup at a time, depending on your food processor). Dump into a large mixing bowl and add remaining ingredients. Mix thoroughly.
2. Roll dough into small balls and then roll each ball in confectioners' sugar. Store in the refrigerator for about 2 weeks.

Walnut Clusters

Simply walnuts and chocolate. So easy, so delicious.

MAKES 2 CUPS OF CANDY.

Ingredients

2 cups walnut pieces   8 ounces chocolate, chopped

Directions

1. Line a baking sheet with parchment paper. Arrange walnut pieces in small clumps across the baking sheet.
2. In a double boiler, melt the chocolate. Use a spoon to scoop melted chocolate onto each clump. Place in the refrigerator for about 30 minutes.

{ Resources }

Wholesome Sweeteners

www.wholesomesweeteners.com

This site sells organic, non-GMO corn syrup, sugar, and stevia.

Barry Farm

www.barryfarm.com

At this site you'll find reasonably priced high quality natural candy-making ingredients, including candy colorings and flavor oils.

An Occasional Chocolate

www.anoccasionalchocolate.com

Great resource for organic chocolate, raw chocolate, and sugar-free chocolate.

Flavorganics

www.flavorganics.com

This site carries a wide range of organic flavorings and extracts.

Maggie's Naturals

www.maggiesnaturals.com

This company sells all-natural, gluten-free food dyes.

Swerve Sweetener

www.swervesweetener.com

Swerve is a natural sweetener that does not raise blood sugar levels and has a 1:1 ratio to regular cane sugar.

Confectionary House

www.confectionaryhouse.com

Look here for candy thermometers, candy cups, candy boxes, and much more.

Vitacost

www.vitacost.com

You can find unbleached parchment paper here, and you can also search specifically for non-GMO ingredients.

{ Recipe Index }

Applet Candies, 66

Apricot-Orange Balls, 106

Black Licorice Twists, 71

Brandy Balls, 107

Butterscotch Candy, 54

Candied Orange Peels, 94

Candy Corn, 84

Candy-Coated Nuts, 96

Caramels

  Coconut Milk Caramels, 38

  Salted Caramels, 34

Caramel Corn, 44

  Peanut Butter Caramel Corn, 47

  Spiced Caramel Corn, 46

Caramelized Mixed Nuts, 97

Cherry Cordials, 10

Chocolate Caramel Peanut Butter Candy Bars, 29

Chocolate Cheesecake Bon Bons, 21

Chocolate Coconut Candy Bars, 2

Chocolate Peanut Butter Balls, 5

Chocolate-Dipped Fruit Skewers, 98

Chocolate-Dipped Honeycomb, 4

Chocolate-Dipped Pretzel Rods, 8

Cinnamon Hard Candies, 50

Citrus Hard Candy, 53

Citrus Pate de Fruit, 79

Coconut Clouds, 68

Coconut Milk Caramels, 38

Coconut Milk Truffles, 18

Coconut Oil Peppermint Patties, 24

Crystallized Ginger, 92

Dates Stuffed with Goat Cheese and Chocolate, 100

Divinity, 83

Dream Bars, 9

Dried Cherry and Chocolate Balls, 103

Fruit Leather, 93

Fudge

  Mocha Fudge, 12

  Peanut Butter Fudge, 14

  White Chocolate Peppermint Fudge, 15

Gummy Candies, 72

Hazelnut Rocher Truffles, 20

Homemade Marshmallows, 74

Honey Lemon Ginger Drops, 55

Maple Nut Brittle, 58

Marzipan, 76

Mocha Fudge, 12

Mocha Meringue Bark, 70

Opera Creams, 77

Orange Creams, 26

Pate de Fruit

Citrus Pate de Fruit, 79

Raspberry Pate de Fruit, 78

Simple Jame Pate de Fruit, 80

Peanut Butter Caramel Corn , 47

Peanut Butter Cups, 6

Peanut Butter Fudge, 14

Pecan Pralines, 99

Pecan Toffee, 40

Penuchi, 28

Peppermint Candy Canes, 60

Peppermint Patties, 22

   Coconut Oil Peppermint Patties, 24

Potato Candy, 82

Raisin Clusters, 102

Raspberry Pate de Fruit, 78

Rock Candy, 62

Salt Water Taffy, 41

Salted Caramels, 34

Sesame Halvah, 88

Simple Jam Pate de Fruit, 80

Spiced Caramel Corn, 46

Sugar Plums, 104

Truffles, 16

   Coconut Milk Truffles, 18

   Hazelnut Rocher Truffles, 20

Vinegar Candy, 57

Walnut Clusters, 108

White Chocolate Peppermint Fudge,
   15

{ Food Allergy Index }

Below are recipes that are gluten-free or dairy-free, or could easily be made as such. Be sure to check labels for all ingredients, as gluten and dairy can pop up in unexpected places. For example, confectioners' sugar, baking powder, and cornstarch sometimes contain gluten, and chocolate chips often contain dairy.

GLUTEN-FREE RECIPES

Applet Candies, 66

Apricot-Orange Balls, 106

Brandy Balls, 107

Butterscotch Candy, 54

Candied Orange Peels, 94

Candy Corn, 84

Candy-Coated Nuts, 96

Caramel Corn, 44

    Peanut Butter Caramel Corn, 47

    Spiced Caramel Corn, 46

Caramelized Mixed Nuts, 97

Cherry Cordials, 10

Chocolate Caramel Peanut Butter Candy Bars, 29

Chocolate Cheesecake Bon Bons, 21

Chocolate Coconut Candy Bars, 2

Chocolate Peanut Butter Balls, 5

Chocolate-Dipped Fruit Skewers, 98

Chocolate-Dipped Honeycomb, 4

Cinnamon Hard Candies, 50

Citrus Hard Candy, 53

Citrus Pate de Fruit, 79

Coconut Clouds, 68

Coconut Milk Caramels , 38

Coconut Milk Truffles, 18

Coconut Oil Peppermint Patties, 24

Crystallized Ginger, 92

Dates Stuffed with Goat Cheese and Chocolate, 100

Divinity, 83

Dried Cherry and Chocolate Balls, 103

Fruit Leather, 93

Fudge

    Mocha Fudge, 12

    Peanut Butter Fudge, 14

    White Chocolate Peppermint Fudge, 15

Gummy Candies, 72

Homemade Marshmallows, 74

Honey Lemon Ginger Drops, 55

Maple Nut Brittle, 58

Marzipan, 76

Mocha Fudge, 12

Mocha Meringue Bark, 70

Opera Creams, 77

Orange Creams, 26

Pate de Fruit

   Citrus Pate de Fruit, 79

   Raspberry Pate de Fruit, 78

   Simple Jame Pate de Fruit, 80

Peanut Butter Caramel Corn , 47

Peanut Butter Cups, 6

Peanut Butter Fudge, 14

Pecan Pralines, 99

Pecan Toffee, 40

Penuchi, 28

Peppermint Candy Canes, 60

Peppermint Patties, 22

   Coconut Oil Peppermint Patties, 24

Potato Candy, 82

Raisin Clusters, 102

Raspberry Pate de Fruit, 78

Rock Candy, 62

Salt Water Taffy, 41

Salted Caramels, 34

Sesame Halvah, 88

Simple Jam Pate de Fruit, 80

Spiced Caramel Corn, 46

Sugar Plums, 104

Truffles, 16

   Coconut Milk Truffles, 18

Vinegar Candy, 57

Walnut Clusters, 108

White Chocolate Peppermint Fudge, 15

DAIRY-FREE RECIPES

When milk, cream, or sweetened condensed milk are called for in these recipes, use coconut milk or coconut sweetened condensed milk (page xiv). Use coconut oil instead of butter. Use dairy-free chocolate.

Applet Candies, 66

Apricot-Orange Balls, 106

Candied Orange Peels, 94

Candy-Coated Nuts, 96

Caramel Corn, 44

   Peanut Butter Caramel Corn, 47

   Spiced Caramel Corn, 46

Cherry Cordials, 10

Chocolate Cheesecake Bon Bons, 21

Chocolate Coconut Candy Bars, 2

Chocolate Peanut Butter Balls, 5

Chocolate-Dipped Fruit Skewers, 98

Chocolate-Dipped Honeycomb, 4

Chocolate-Dipped Pretzel Rods, 8

Cinnamon Hard Candies, 50

Citrus Hard Candy, 53

Citrus Pate de Fruit, 79

Coconut Clouds, 68

Coconut Milk Caramels, 38

Coconut Milk Truffles, 18

Coconut Oil Peppermint Patties, 24

Crystallized Ginger, 92

Dates Stuffed with Goat Cheese and
Chocolate, 100

Divinity, 83

Dream Bars, 9

Dried Cherry and Chocolate Balls, 103

Fruit Leather, 93

Fudge

    Mocha Fudge, 12

    Peanut Butter Fudge, 14

    White Chocolate Peppermint Fudge,
    15

Gummy Candies, 72

Homemade Marshmallows, 74

Honey Lemon Ginger Drops, 55

Maple Nut Brittle, 58

Marzipan, 76

Mocha Fudge, 12

Mocha Meringue Bark, 70

Orange Creams, 26

Pate de Fruit

    Citrus Pate de Fruit, 79

    Raspberry Pate de Fruit, 78

    Simple Jame Pate de Fruit, 80

Peanut Butter Caramel Corn , 47

Peanut Butter Cups, 6

Peanut Butter Fudge, 14

Peppermint Candy Canes, 60

Peppermint Patties

    Coconut Oil Peppermint Patties, 24

Potato Candy, 82

Raisin Clusters, 102

Raspberry Pate de Fruit, 78

Rock Candy, 62

Sesame Halvah, 88

Simple Jam Pate de Fruit, 80

Spiced Caramel Corn, 46

Sugar Plums, 104

Truffles

    Coconut Milk Truffles, 18

Walnut Clusters, 108

White Chocolate Peppermint Fudge,
15

{ Conversion Charts }

METRIC AND IMPERIAL CONVERSIONS
(These conversions are rounded for convenience)

Ingredient	Cups/Tablespoons/ Teaspoons	Ounces	Grams/Milliliters
Butter	1 cup=16 tablespoons= 2 sticks	8 ounces	230 grams
Cream cheese	1 tablespoon	0.5 ounce	14.5 grams
Cornstarch	1 tablespoon	0.3 ounce	8 grams
Flour, all-purpose	1 cup/1 tablespoon	4.5 ounces/0.3 ounce	125 grams/8 grams
Flour, whole wheat	1 cup	4 ounces	120 grams
Fruit, dried	1 cup	4 ounces	120 grams
Fruits, chopped	1 cup	5 to 7 ounces	145 to 200 grams
Fruits, puréed	1 cup	8.5 ounces	245 grams
Honey, maple syrup, or corn syrup	1 tablespoon	.75 ounce	20 grams
Liquids: cream, milk, water, or juice	1 cup	8 fluid ounces	240 milliliters
Oats	1 cup	5.5 ounces	150 grams
Salt	1 teaspoon	0.2 ounce	6 grams
Spices: cinnamon, cloves, ginger, or nutmeg (ground)	1 teaspoon	0.2 ounce	5 milliliters
Sugar, brown, firmly packed	1 cup	7 ounces	200 grams
Sugar, white	1 cup/1 tablespoon	7 ounces/0.5 ounce	200 grams/12.5 grams
Vanilla extract	1 teaspoon	0.2 ounce	4 grams